To Teresa

May God continue to bless you in ways you have yet to imagine.

REMINDERS FOR GRINDERS

REMINDERS FOR GRINDERS

THIS BOOK IS PRESENTED TO

BY

ON THE OCCASION OF

DATE

REMINDERS FOR GRINDERS

REMINDERS FOR GRINDERS

Copyright © 2019 by Dana Bennett of Bennett Publishing House

All rights reserved. *No part of this book may be reproduced, stored in a retrieval system, or transmitted in any form or by any means, electronic, mechanical photocopying, recording, or otherwise, without written consent of the publisher except in the case of brief quotations in critical articles or reviews.*

Library of Congress – Catalogued in Publication Data

ISBN 13: 9781693756610

Printed in the United States of America

Book Publishing Assistance:
Jabez Books Writer's Agency
www.JabezBooks.com
(A Division of Clark's Consultant Group)

Cover designed by Christina Runnels
Genesis One Designs

Scripture quotations are from various version of the Bible

ACKNOWLEDGEMENTS

This book would not be in your hands had it not been for the people in my life who push and inspire me. I am forever grateful for the people God placed in my life. I have an amazing tribe. I would like to thank Dr. Shirley Clark who literally pushed this devotional out of my spirit and onto paper. Thank you for believing in me and being patient with me during this process, but most of all, thank you for not allowing me to postpone destiny any longer. Dr. Clark, you are a true midwife and miracle worker.

A huge thank you to my better half, Pastor Ken Bennett. Since the first day we met, you have been speaking to me about my purpose and the gifts on my life. You encourage me, pray for me, and believe in me in ways that make a difference in who I am. I am grateful for your love, guidance and support. Because of your love, I am better.

I would also like to thank my graphic designer and photographer, Christina Runnels. This multi-talented, creative phenom is always so gracious with her time and talent. She just gets me and never misses with her designs. Thank you, my sister, and may everything your hands touch be blessed.

REMINDERS FOR GRINDERS

Last, but not least, I want to thank the persons who most inspire me to pray: my mother, Vanessa K. Ray, and my pastors, Bishop Sherman C. Gee Allen and Co-Pastor Otonya Eskridge Allen. My mother introduced me to Jesus at a young age, and I have watched her pray and trust God my entire life. What a beautiful legacy to leave your children. I pray I live out every one of your prayers for my life. My pastors restored my faith in people and the church. I came to them broken-hearted and skeptical. Through watching their lives, I have hope and know that angels really do walk among us. I so appreciate how you selflessly pour into others and continue to live by faith, so that others might believe. Your prayers and love have held me and my family together. I am eternally grateful.

INTRODUCTION

Why *Reminders for Grinders*? First, what is a grinder? A grinder is anyone who has a vision to do something great and doesn't mind putting in the work both naturally and spiritually to make it happen. I am a mother, wife, student, business woman, and pastor. I know how challenging it can be to set out to do something great and hit obstacles along the way. This is why in this book I am sharing some of my favorite scriptures and quotes that I go to when I need encouragement and focus. Nothing magnificent happens overnight and without sacrifice, determination, favor, and prayer. My hope is that these pages inspire you to never give up on what God has placed in your heart. You are already equipped to be great now just keep grinding!

REMINDERS FOR GRINDERS

DAY 1

*Then the Lord answered me and said:
"Write the vision and make it plain on tables, that
he may run who reads it."
Habakkuk 2:2 (NKJ)*

The discipline of writing something down is
the first step toward making it happen.
 - Lee Iacocca

~THOUGHT FOR THE DAY~

Getting it out of your head and onto paper forces you to do more than just dream about it. Now you must take action.

PRAYER

Father God, thank You for every gift You have placed inside of me. Help me to see the vision You have for me and how I can use these gifts for the Kingdom of God. Help me to write out the vision and put action to what it is You have called me to do. Like Nehemiah, give me a mind to build. Show me how to make this vision plain, so that others that You send to help me can clearly see the vision and know how they can help. And while I am sharing the vision with others, never let me lose sight of what You have given me to do, even when it seems as if the vision is slow to come to pass. Lord, thank You for entrusting me with this vision; now I ask for Your divine power to help me carry it out to Your Glory. In Jesus' name, I pray. And it is so!

REMINDERS FOR GRINDERS

REFLECTION

REMINDERS FOR GRINDERS

REFLECTION

DAY 2

*Ask and it will be given to you;
seek and you will find; knock and the
door will be opened to you.
Matthew 7:7 (NIV)*

You create your opportunities by asking for them.
- **Patty Hansen**

~THOUGHT FOR THE DAY~

A closed mouth does not get fed. Do yourself a favor and ask for what you want. You would be surprised at how many doors open as a result of a simple request.

PRAYER

Lord God, I come to You alone asking for what I need because I know that You are Jehovah-Jireh - a strong and faithful provider. Your word declares that if I ask, it will be given; if I seek, I would find, and if I knock, the doors would be opened. Your word also says that when we pray according to Your will, You hear us. Teach me, oh, Lord, what things to ask for in this season, and I thank You in advance for open doors and answered prayers. Even now God, I know You are setting up divine connections and meetings, so that every need and request I have before You shall be answered. May every open door advance Your Kingdom agenda. I praise You now confident that it is already done. In Jesus' name, I pray. And it is so!

REMINDERS FOR GRINDERS

REFLECTION

REMINDERS FOR GRINDERS

REFLECTION

DAY 3

*Jesus looked at them and said,
"With man this is impossible, but with God
all things are possible."
Matthew 19:26 (NIV)*

"There are no boundaries - only possibilities.
- **Sakyong Mipham Rinpoche**

~THOUGHT FOR THE DAY~

I am limited; God is not. I tie His hands when I place my limits on a limitless God.

PRAYER

Oh faithful and mighty God, I know that nothing is too hard for You. You spoke and the earth came into form. You breathed and man came to life. Surely any need I have or obstacle in my way must bow to Your great glory. I know that in my own strength I would fail and fumble, but You, oh God, are able to do all things well. Move on my behalf, Lord, and allow me to experience what man deems impossible. I take the limits off of my thinking and off of You, oh God, knowing You can do anything but fail. I stand firm on Your reputation and declare that every mountain is moved, every enemy is defeated and every need is met. In Jesus, name. And it is so, and cannot be otherwise!

REMINDERS FOR GRINDERS

REFLECTION

… REMINDERS FOR GRINDERS

REFLECTION

DAY 4

*You will keep him in perfect
peace, whose mind is stayed on You.
Because he trusts You.
Isaiah 26:3 (NKJ)*

Nothing can disturb your peace of mind
unless you allow it to.
- **Roy T. Bennett**

~THOUGHT FOR THE DAY~

If I am fretting, I know my mind has been in places it should not wander.

PRAYER

Father, I thank You on today for peace - peace with God and peace with man. I thank You that my mind is at rest because I choose to think on Your goodness, kindness, mercy and majesty. I give my thoughts over to You asking that You help me to think on whatsoever is pure, good and lovely. God, I trust You, and I refuse to lean unto my own understanding. I trust that no matter what this day may bring, You are in control, so there is no need to worry, be anxious, or frustrated. I will walk this day in the divine peace of God. In Jesus' name, and it is so!

REMINDERS FOR GRINDERS

REFLECTION

REMINDERS FOR GRINDERS

REFLECTION

REMINDERS FOR GRINDERS

DAY 5

Create in me a pure heart, O God,
and renew a steadfast spirit within me.
Psalm 51:10 (NIV)

When your intentions are
pure, so too will be your success.
- Charles F. Glassman MD

~THOUGHT FOR THE DAY~

Sometimes we are delayed not because what we are doing is not good, but because our motive is tainted.

PRAYER

Father, search my heart and remove anything that is not like You or stands in opposition to Your will. Let me not be puffed up with pride or do things to create fame and fortune for my name sake, but let everything I do bring You glory. You alone are deserving. Do not let me be guilty of impure motives or agendas, but let my efforts serve You. I yield my will to Yours, oh God. You lead and guide me, so that I do not fall into making an idol of myself or my works. Let my heart stay right before you always so that my ways may be blessed. In Jesus, name, Amen.

REMINDERS FOR GRINDERS

REFLECTION

REMINDERS FOR GRINDERS

REFLECTION

DAY 6

For which of you, intending to build a tower, does not sit down first and count the cost, whether he has enough to finish it— lest, after he has laid the foundation, and is not able to finish, all who see it begin to mock him, saying, 'This man began to build and was not able to finish'? Luke 14:28-30 (NKJ)

The reason many people fail is not for lack of vision but for lack of resolve and resolve is born out of counting the cost. - **Robert H. Goddard**

~THOUGHT FOR THE DAY~

Most count the money they will make but not the money they will lose, the hours of sleep they will miss, the friends that will leave, and so they give in to doubt right before earning the prize. Every dream, every vision costs something and for most of us...it will cost everything.

PRAYER

Heavenly Father, make me wise. Help me to count the costs before I set out on this journey to fulfill my calling. Let me not get weary in well doing along the way, but let me remember that obstacles are a necessary part of the course, and you are bigger than anything I will face. Lord make up the difference on anything I failed to factor into this journey, and I thank You in advance for the return I will receive on my investment and sacrifice. You be glorified in this endeavor. In Jesus' name, Amen.

REMINDERS FOR GRINDERS

REFLECTION

REMINDERS FOR GRINDERS

REFLECTION

DAY 7

For just as the body without the spirit is dead, so also faith without works is dead.
James 2:26 (NKJ)

Faith and works are bound up in the same bundle. He that obeys God trusts God; and he that trusts God obeys God. He that is without faith is without works; and he that is without works is without faith.
- Charles Spurgeon

~THOUGHT FOR THE DAY~

Real faith always has a corresponding action. You cannot say God said go, yet your feet fail to move.

PRAYER

Dear Lord, I have faith in You; help me to take action on what I believe. Help me to not just speak on what You will do, but allow me to partner with You in faith and begin to move. Help me to not just be busy, but to put my energy and efforts into things that flow in alignment with what You have called me to do. Let me not just be a hearer of the Word, but let me be a doer also. Let my feet move because You said go, and let my heart believe because You said it is so. Spur me on to good works that testify of my faith. In Jesus' name, Amen!

REMINDERS FOR GRINDERS

REFLECTION

REFLECTION

DAY 8

*Have I not commanded you? Be
strong and courageous. Do not be afraid; do not
be discouraged, for the LORD your God will
be with you wherever you go.
Joshua 1:9 (NIV)*

I learned that courage was not the absence of fear, but the triumph over it. The brave man is not he who does not feel afraid, but he who conquers that fear.
– Nelson Mandela

~THOUGHT FOR THE DAY~

Take courage in knowing that even in your darkest hours, the Lord is still yet with you. He commanded us to be strong and courageous because He knew there would be moments where we would be tempted to walk away because of fear. I can stand my ground knowing He is with me.

REMINDERS FOR GRINDERS

PRAYER

Heavely Father, I know that you are always near, even in the darkest moments. I will do as you have commanded and not succumb to fear and doubt, but I will courageously stand on Your promises. You are bigger than any problem or situation I may face, and so I endure hardship like a good solider knowing You are with me. There is no place that I can go where You are not with me, and because of this I can triumph and stand bravely in the face of things that make most crumble. I praise You now for victory! In Jesus' name, and it is so!

REMINDERS FOR GRINDERS

REFLECTION

REMINDERS FOR GRINDERS

REFLECTION

DAY 9

*Let us not become weary in doing
good, for at the proper time we will reap
a harvest if we do not give up.
Galatians 6:9 (NIV)*

The two hardest tests on the spiritual
road are the patience to wait for the right moment
and the courage not to be disappointed
with what we encounter.
- Paulo Coelho

~THOUGHT FOR THE DAY~

We must fight against the urge to be disappointed when things do not turn out the way we think they should, especially when we have done all we know to do. It takes courage and faith to keep watering ground that has yet to produce...but know that a harvest is on its way.

PRAYER

Heavenly Father, You are Lord of everything. There is none like You. I trust You with my life and You have never let me down. Therefore, as I sow seeds in kingdom endeavors, I am completely confident that You will bless me in due season. I have no reservations about this, so I keep my eyes on You and my hands on the plow. When the road gets tough, I will remember the promises of Your Word. My best days are before me. And it is so. In Jesus' name, Amen!

REMINDERS FOR GRINDERS

REFLECTION

REMINDERS FOR GRINDERS

REFLECTION

DAY 10

*For I know the plans I have for you,
plans to prosper you and not to harm you, plans to
give you hope and a future.
Jeremiah 29:11 (NIV)*

A clear vision, backed by definite plans,
gives you a tremendous feeling of confidence
and personal power.
- **Brian Tracy**

~THOUGHT FOR THE DAY~

When we were born God had a prophetic assignment already attached to our lives. So never allow setbacks and challenges to derail you from believing that your prophetic destiny is not coming to pass.

PRAYER

Father God, You are in control, and I know that You have wonderful things in store for my life. I may not see the end, but I know You have already set each day in motion even before I was born. You know my beginning from my end, and for that I am grateful. Nothing takes You by surprise, so I rest in Your sovereignty. Your Word declares that man makes his plans, but it is You, Lord, who orders our steps. Continue to lead and guide me toward the path of prosperity and righteousness. In Jesus' name, Amen!

REMINDERS FOR GRINDERS

REFLECTION

REMINDERS FOR GRINDERS

REFLECTION

DAY 11

*Commit to the Lord whatever you do,
and He will establish your plans.
Proverbs 16:3 (NIV)*

Motivation is what gets you started.
Commitment is what keeps you going
- Jim Rohn

~THOUGHT FOR THE DAY~

I commit all that I do to the Lord, so He can then partner with me in making it a success. He has no obligation to uphold what He is not a part of.

PRAYER

Lord, I commit all my works to You. My life, business, family, and ministry all belong to You. You get the glory out of it all. I take no credit for any good thing in my life for it is You who causes my plans to succeed. Father give increase as You see fit knowing what my character can handle. Show me how to let all that I do benefit the Kingdom of God and Your desires for my life. In Jesus' name, and it is so.

REMINDERS FOR GRINDERS

REFLECTION

REMINDERS FOR GRINDERS

REFLECTION

DAY 12

And we know that all things work together for good to those who love God, to those who are the called according to His purpose.
Romans 8:28 (NKJ)

I never lose. I either win or I learn.
- Nelson Mandela

~THOUGHT FOR THE DAY~

Even the stuff that hurts is making me better. I don't fight it anymore; I ask what am I to learn from this.

PRAYER

God, You are so incredible. I am in constant awe of Your greatness. It is Your loving kindness and sovereignty that works all things together for my good. You cause me to triumph over every plan of the enemy. I have no need to worry about my future because You know my beginning from my end. Nothing happens in my life that You do not allow, and I rest in Your trusted plan. You are a very present help in times of trouble, and You always provide a way of escape. I thank You for Your goodness and mercy that are new for me each day. In Jesus' name, Amen!

REMINDERS FOR GRINDERS

REFLECTION

REMINDERS FOR GRINDERS

REFLECTION

DAY 13

*But seek ye first the kingdom of God,
and his righteousness; and all these things
shall be added unto you.
Matthew 6:33 (KJV)*

The seeker always finds what
he seeks simply because of constant
attention and perseverance.
Anonymous

~THOUGHT FOR THE DAY~

Don't be so worried about amassing earthly treasures that you forfeit your place with God. If we are about our Father's business, He is faithful to see about ours.

PRAYER

Father, You are the great giver of life and the creator of all things. As I set my heart daily to seek You, my life will never be the same. My heart constantly pants after you and in your presence is fulness of joy. I know that the road that I have been destined to take having you by my side is one of the greatest gifts in my life. I will forever praise and exalt You. Let my life be a reflection of Your goodness that others might be drawn to You. God, I love You more and more each day. In Jesus' name, Amen!

REFLECTION

REMINDERS FOR GRINDERS

REFLECTION

DAY 14

Be anxious for nothing; but in everything by prayer and supplication with thanksgiving let your requests be made known unto God.
Philippians 4:6 (NKJ)

We should not fret for what is past, nor should we be anxious about the future; men of discernment deal only with the present moment.
- Chanakya

~THOUGHT FOR THE DAY~

I will not worry in God's direction. Either I trust Him or I don't.

PRAYER

Lord God, I come to You laying every burden at your feet. I thank You that You already know what I have need of, and I trust that You are already working on my behalf. I dare not worry in Your direction and cancel out the very faith in which I pray, but I come to You knowing that You are the rewarder of them that diligently seek You. Father, my life is in Your hands, and I will not be overcome with anxiety and worry. You make all things come together for my good and I rest in knowing You are ever faithful. To worry is to doubt Your goodness, faithfulness and omniscience. I choose to believe that You are Lord and all things must bow to You, even the spirit of worry. I set my mind on You and will stand still and see the salvation of the Lord. In Jesus' name, Amen!

REMINDERS FOR GRINDERS

REFLECTION

REMINDERS FOR GRINDERS

REFLECTION

DAY 15

For as he thinketh in his heart, so is he.
Proverbs 23:7 (KJV)

The world as we have created it is a
process of our thinking. It cannot be changed without
changing our thinking.
- **Albert Einstein**

~THOUGHT FOR THE DAY~

I am only as good as my thoughts. If I do not like what I see in the mirror, I need first to change my thoughts.

PRAYER

Lord, help me to see myself as You see me. Do not let me sabotage who I am with negative thinking. I come against poor self-image and poor self-esteem. I declare that I am fearfully and wonderfully made in the image of God. I cast down any thought sent from the enemy that suggests that I am not loved, forgiven, anointed, whole and free. I thank You for the liberty that comes from a relationship with You. Now that I am a new creature, I thank You that old things are passed away and all things are made new in my life. Take my mind and transform my thoughts until I think with the mind of Christ. I thank You for a renewed outlook on who I am. In Jesus' name, Amen!

REMINDERS FOR GRINDERS

REFLECTION

REMINDERS FOR GRINDERS

REFLECTION

DAY 16

*But remember the LORD your
God, for it is he who gives you the ability to produce
wealth, and so confirms his covenant, which he
swore to your ancestors, as it is today.
Deuteronomy 8:18 (NIV)*

God has ordained the blessing of
prosperity to work through faith in Him and
therein lies the greatest wealth.
- Jim Ballew

~THOUGHT FOR THE DAY~

Part of doing anything well is having the confidence to know that you can. So many of us fail to create wealth because we do not believe that it is a God-given ability. We believe it only belongs to some; we all have the ability to create wealth, it is whether or not we exercise it and learn to master it that matters.

PRAYER

Father God, thank You for equipping me with the ability to create wealth. I honor You by not squandering or doubting that gift, but by operating in what You have already designed me to do. I was created in Your image and Your Word declares You are rich in houses and land, so I declare, so am I. I believe that I will be the lender and not the borrower, the head and not the tail simply because it is in my divine DNA to have wealth. I decree generational wealth on my family and downline. Lord, I ask that You remove any mental or spiritual blocks that would stunt my creativity, but I release witty ideas, inventions, and solutions that would generate money in the earth. I thank You that wealth is my portion and I activate my faith to receive it. In Jesus' name, and it is so!

REMINDERS FOR GRINDERS

REFLECTION

REMINDERS FOR GRINDERS

REFLECTION

REMINDERS FOR GRINDERS

DAY 17

I have come that they might have life,
and that they might have it more abundantly.
John 10:10 (KJV)

When you focus on being a
blessing, God makes sure that you are
always blessed in abundance.
- Joel Osteen

~THOUGHT FOR THE DAY~

I am not just here to live, but I am here to live in an amazing way that speaks well of who my God is.

PRAYER

Jesus, You are my rock and salvation. Thank You for giving me abundant life. As I walk with You daily, You shine light in the dark places to protect me from evil. Your precious Holy Spirit is with me as well, therefore, I delight to do Your will. My heart is forever anchored in Your goodness and mercy. Lord, continue to surround me with Your grace as I celebrate all that You have done in my life. And I also thank You that Your love is so great in my life that I am empowered to do incredible things. I will be forever grateful. In Jesus' name, Amen!

REMINDERS FOR GRINDERS

REFLECTION

REMINDERS FOR GRINDERS

REFLECTION

DAY 18

Now faith is the substance of things hoped for, the evidence of things not seen.
Hebrews 11:1 (KJV)

When you do business with people you need money. When you do business with God you need faith. Faith is the currency of the Kingdom of God.
- **Reinhard Bonnke**

~THOUGHT FOR THE DAY~

I do not worry about what I cannot see. Faith tells me what is true, not my senses.

PRAYER

Lord, my hope is in You. This day I walk in insurmountable faith. I have mountain moving faith, and no weapon formed against me will prosper. The Word declares that the just shall live by faith, and I am righteous, therefore, I release in the earth what I need and want. My mouth is an instrument of faith, which I choose to release kingdom endeavors and projects into the earth. Thank You, God, for being able to do exceeding abundantly above all that I can ask or think. This is my day of manifestation. In the Matchless Name of Jesus, Amen.

REMINDERS FOR GRINDERS

REFLECTION

REMINDERS FOR GRINDERS

REFLECTION

DAY 19

*The blessing of the Lord, it maketh rich,
and he addeth no sorrow with it.
Proverbs 10:22 (KJV)*

Don't be afraid to
give up the good to go for the great.
- John D. Rockefeller

~THOUGHT FOR THE DAY~

As the Lord blesses you, give yourself permission to enjoy His abundance.

PRAYER

Most precious and gracious God, thank You for loving me and surrounding me with Your goodness. Wherever I go I am blessed. I am blessed going in and blessed going out. I am blessed in the field and I am blessed in the city. Your loving kindness is better than life. I will exalt You above the mountains. There is none that can stop You from blessing Your people. I am a recipient of a never-ending flow of riches, wealth and creativity. I thank You, because You are the One who gives me power to get wealth so that Your kingdom might be established in all the earth. I activate this scripture today and release a vortex of kingdom blessings in my life, my family life, my friends and my church. As long as I live, whatever my hands touch share prosper. In Jesus' name, Amen!

REMINDERS FOR GRINDERS

REFLECTION

REMINDERS FOR GRINDERS

REFLECTION

DAY 20

My brethren, count it all joy when ye fall into divers temptations; Knowing this, that the trying of your faith worketh patience. But let patience have her perfect work, that ye may be perfect and entire, wanting nothing.
James 1:2-4 (KJV)

Trust the process. Your time is coming. Just do the work and the results will handle themselves.
- Tony Gaskins

~THOUGHT FOR THE DAY~

Being successful in life will require a substantial amount of patience. So, don't allow the process to hinder your progress. It is only a moment in time; not your destiny.

PRAYER

God, from everlasting to everlasting, You are my God. Because of this, I have patience and I will not fear the unknown. The earth is the Lord's and fulness thereof. You hold all things in the palm of Your hands; I will not be anxious or fearful of what the enemy can do to me. This day I pull on Your sovereign mercy and grace to guide me through every challenge or opposition I might encounter. I will not wavier under pressure. Instead, I will stand strong knowing that You have the best for me. I am victorious in every way. To God be the glory. In Jesus' glorious name, Amen!

REMINDERS FOR GRINDERS

REFLECTION

REMINDERS FOR GRINDERS

REFLECTION

DAY 21

*Cast thy burden upon the LORD,
and he shall sustain thee: he shall never suffer
the righteous to be moved.
Psalm 55:22 (KJV)*

Happiness is a choice. You can choose to be happy. There's going to be stress in life, but it's your choice whether you let it affect you or not.
- **Valerie Bertinelli**

~THOUGHT FOR THE DAY~

Why carries burdens when you were not ordained to carry them.

PRAYER

Lord, I thank You for being my fortress and sustainer. Whenever I am down, You lift me up. Truly, You are a God that never fails. You are always with me, and I trust You. Every burden or negative circumstance that comes into my life, I quickly reject them and turn them over to You. Thank You for delivering me from every attack and heavy burden that the enemy tries to put on my life to sway me from Your truth. You are the God of miracles. So, I am energized at another level to do supernatural things in this day. I decree it and declare it. In Jesus' name, Amen.

REMINDERS FOR GRINDERS

REFLECTION

REMINDERS FOR GRINDERS

REFLECTION

To contact or book Dana Bennett to speak, please email:

Bookings@DanaRayBennett.com

REMINDERS FOR GRINDERS